THE LONDON COLOURING BOOK

KU-215-985

Buster Books

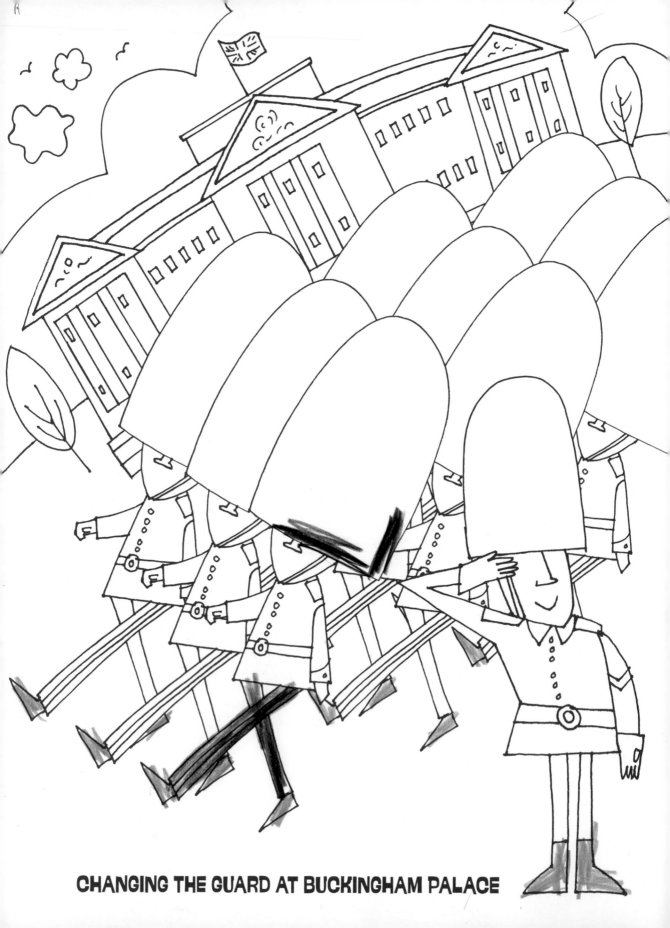

CHANGING THE GUARD AT BUCKINGHAM PALACE

NELSON'S COLUMN
AT TRAFALGAR SQUARE

HENRY VIII AT HAMPTON COURT PALACE

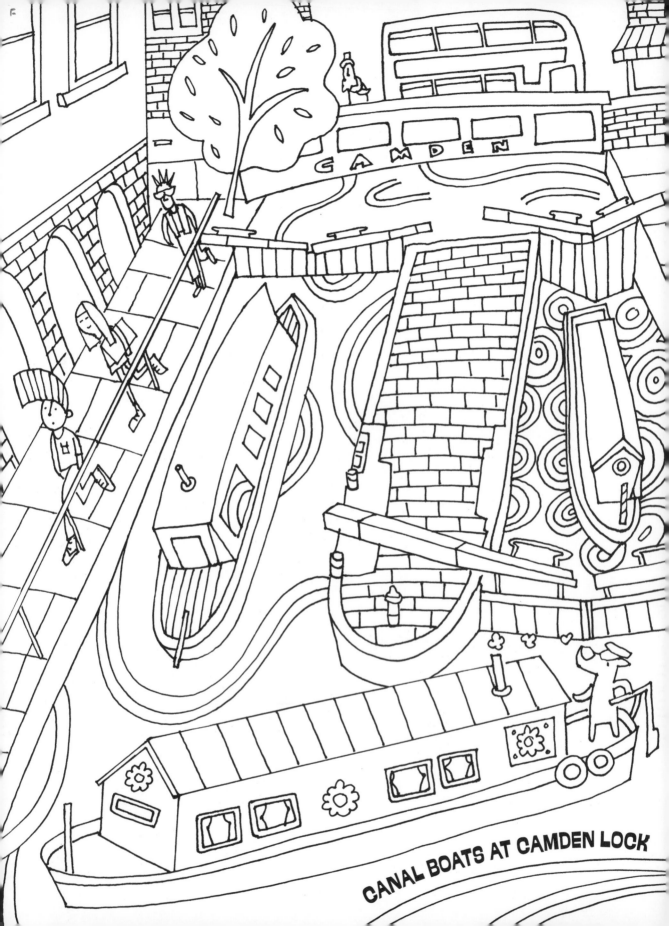

CANAL BOATS AT CAMDEN LOCK

GREENWICH

SIGHTS TO SEE ALONG THE RIVER SIDE

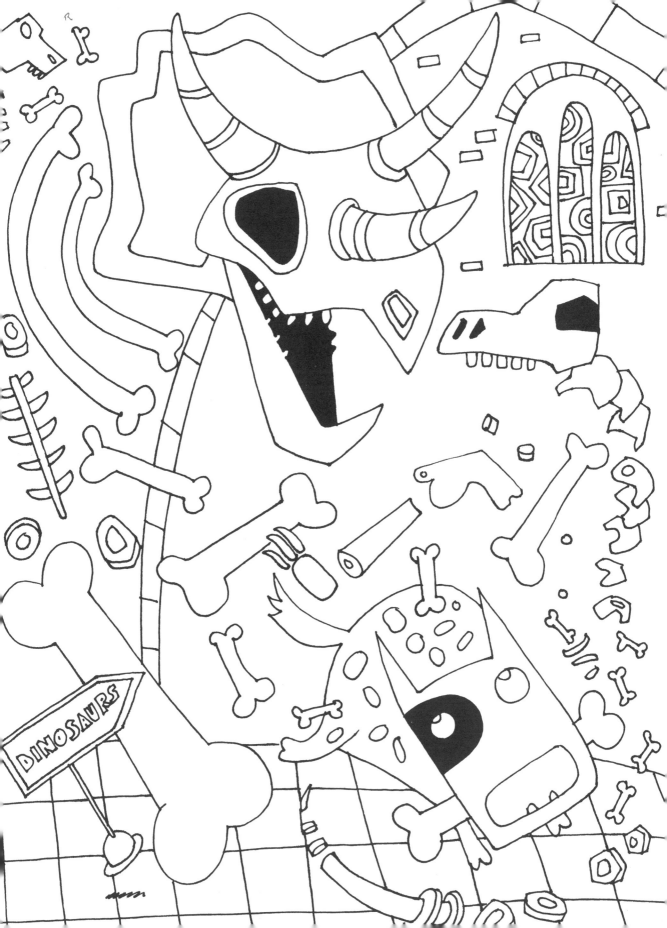

SET SAIL ON THE SERPENTINE
IN HYDE PARK

MAKING WAVES AT WESTMINSTER

TROOPING THE COLOUR

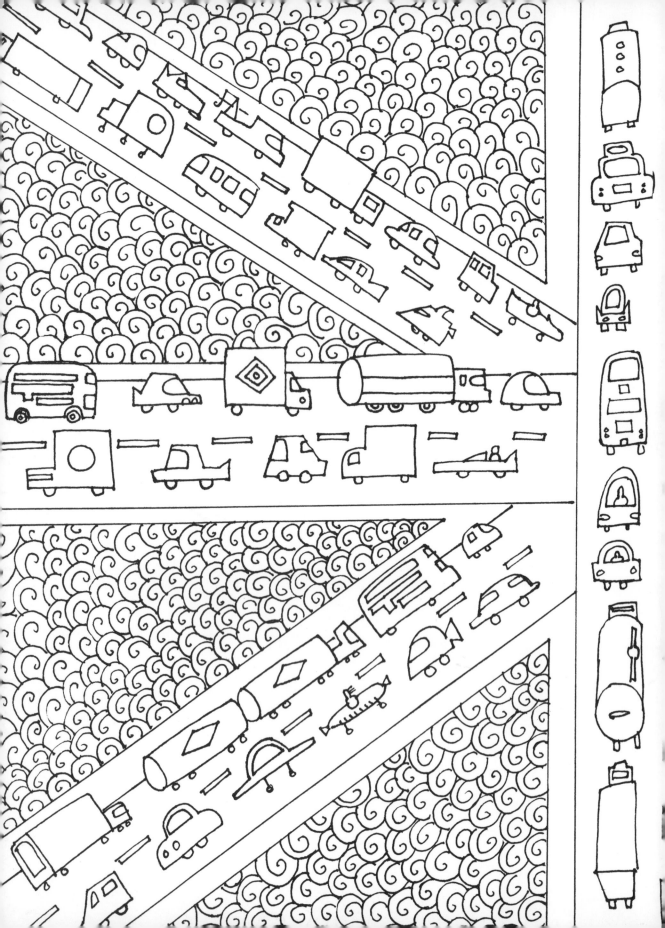

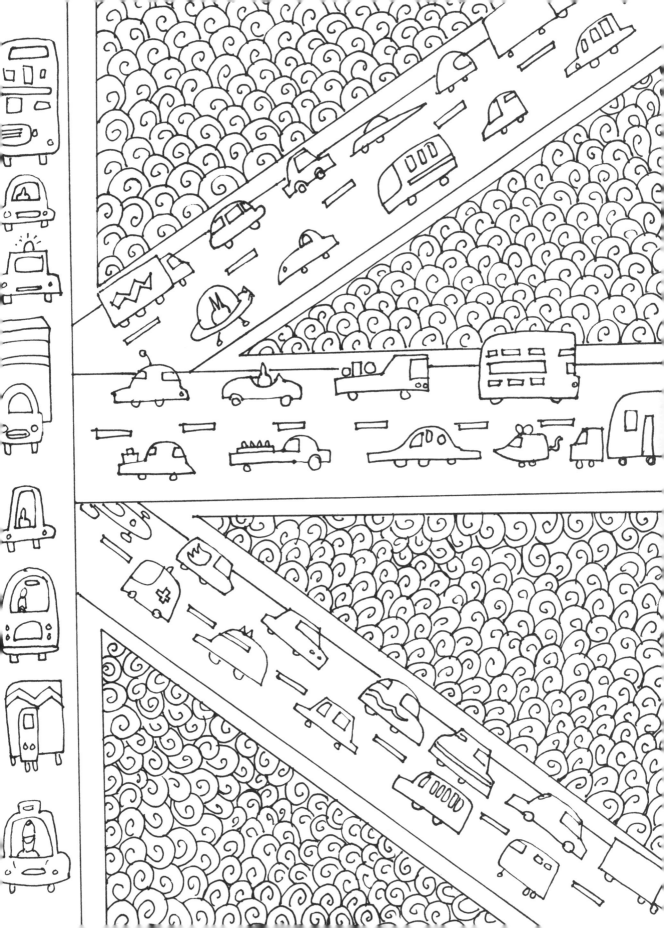

SERVING STRAWBERRIES AT WIMBLEDON

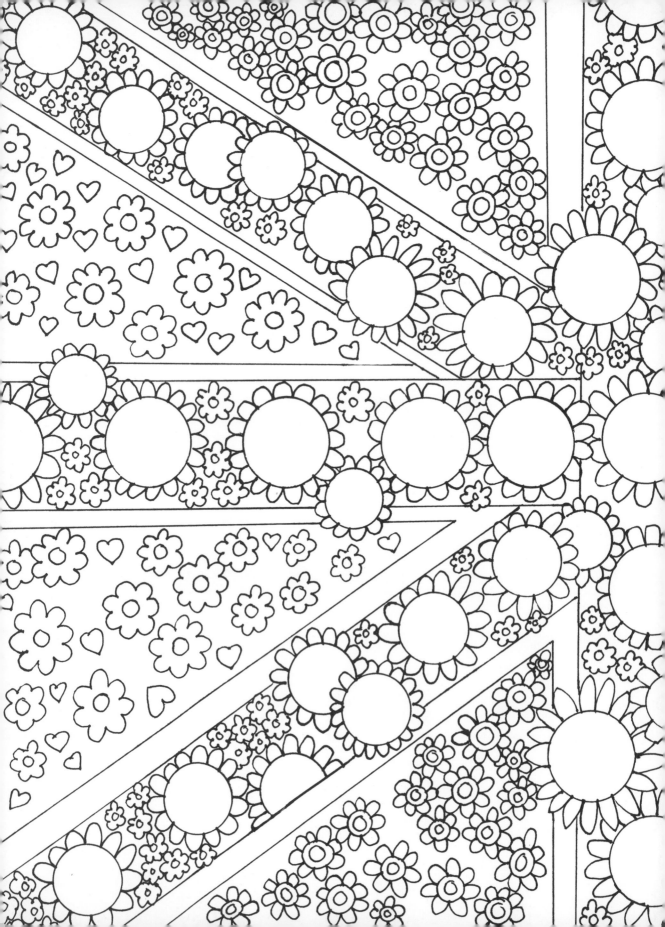

ST PAUL'S CATHEDRAL

THE MONUMENT TO THE GREAT FIRE

GOING FOR GOLD AT THE OLYMPIC PARK

KEW GARDENS HAS FLOWER POWER

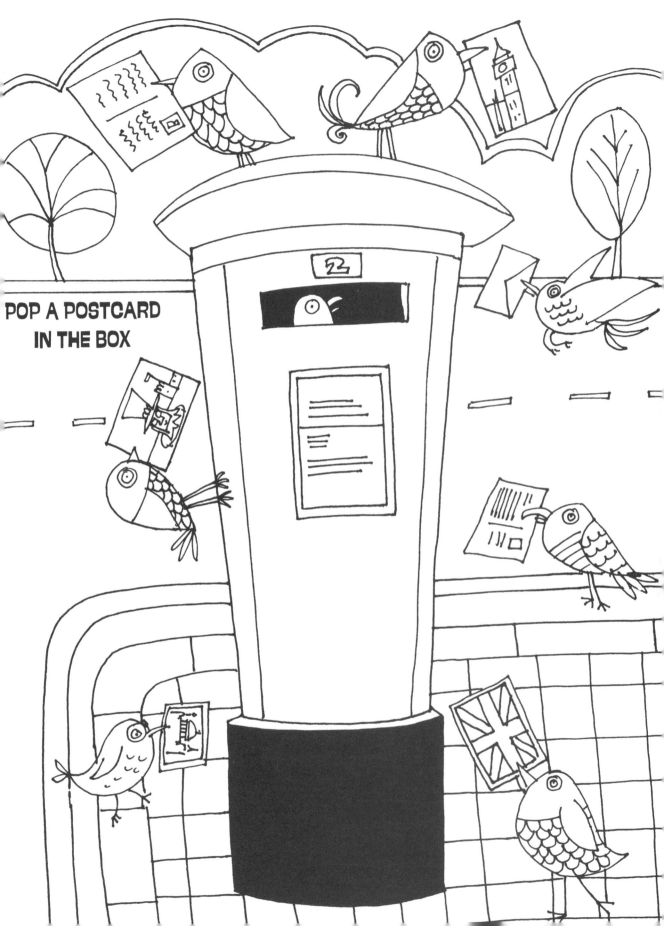

POP A POSTCARD
IN THE BOX

TAKE A PEEK AT THE CROWN JEWELS

EAST MEETS THE WEST END IN CHINA TOWN

First published in Great Britain in 2012 by Buster Books,
an imprint of Michael O'Mara Books Limited,
9 Lion Yard, Tremadoc Road, London SW4 7NQ

Copyright © 2012 Buster Books

A CIP catalogue record for this book is available
from the British Library.

ISBN: 978-1-78055-021-3

2 4 6 8 10 9 7 5 3 1

This book was printed in January 2012 by Shenzhen Wing King Tong
Paper Products Co. Ltd., Shenzhen, Guangdong, China.

Papers used by Michael O'Mara Books are natural, recyclable
products made from wood grown in sustainable forests.
The manufacturing processes conform to the environmental
regulations of the country of origin.

www.busterbooks.co.uk

If you like doodling, visit our doodle website at:
www.doyoudoodle.co.uk